LYNDA CHURILLA

PHILOSOPHY DOG

THE ART OF LIVING WITH MAN'S BEST FRIEND

BY BREON O'FARRELL

UNIVERSE

This book is dedicated to Lord, my first dog

TABLE OF CONTENTS

MARIO TESTINO

IN
THE
BEGINNING

At the age of twenty-five, I took a job as house and office cleaner for Bruce Weber and Nan Bush, a couple who are in the photography and movie businesses. I didn't own a dog then because my life was a mess, and I could barely take care of myself. Nan and Bruce helped me turn my life around.

It was a big deal when they hired me, and I think they did so because their golden retriever, Rowdy, took a liking to me. Rowdy was ten years old when we met, and walking him should have been the best part of the job. But after weeks of meandering around TriBeCa, with me following Rowdy, it became clear that neither of us were happy with this arrangement. Rowdy wanted me to lead him, but my psychology demanded that he be in charge. I was determined to treat Rowdy like royalty because I felt guilty about how I had mistreated and neglected my own childhood dog, Lord. So I allowed Rowdy to run the show. He got his way with everything. I was just an accessory worn at the other end of his leash. Despite his age, Rowdy was still quite vigorous. Nan and Bruce decided to get a puppy to help him grow old happily. The puppy was named Little Bear, but I called him Little Terror because of the number of books he chewed.

An obedience trainer was hired to put an end to Little Bear's chewing, and I was happy to participate in the training sessions. Although a lifelong dog lover, I knew I had plenty to learn. In teaching the pup

the basic obedience commands, I learned that dogs require a particular kind of relationship with humans in order to feel happy and safe. Dogs are pack animals that will follow a leader, and I needed to release my guilty feelings regarding my childhood dog Lord, so I could lead Rowdy and Little Bear toward happier lives, which was easier said than done.

Bruce and Nan were expanding their business and needed to hire additional office cleaners and a cook. I was spending most of my workday with the dogs, and it showed in the dusty floors. I talked with my employers about their expansion, and they suggested I get into the dog business with them as my first client. This idea was brilliant! A surge of enthusiasm engulfed me. I finally felt like I had a meaningful career: I would help busy New Yorkers with their dogs. I read books, watched videos, trained my friends' dogs, and soon discovered a vital common thread: Most dog owners could stand to improve their leadership skills.

I have devised simple guidelines to accomplish this goal. If I can do it, anyone can. When you improve your leadership skills as a dog owner, you will create one of life's most rewarding experiences: being best friend with a good dog. The rest of your life may also change for the better.

LLOYD ZIFF

THE TEACHER'S PET

My career as a dog trainer was all set. But during my first lesson, I failed. Painfully.

Wally was one of my first students—class of '88. His owner was a gentle, compassionate and gifted person. Wally, however, was more than a little bit spoiled. The little dog had chutzpah though, and I liked him straight away. Unfortunately, Wally refused to give me a chance to be his friend. My inexperience didn't help the situation either.

More than anything else, my feelings were hurt because he didn't like me. What had I ever done to him? All dogs liked me, so I wanted to blame him for the tension between us. The truth is, I was not a very good dog trainer at that time. In 1986, I learned to communicate leadership through tough treatment.

This destructive philosophy proved erroneous. Now I teach people to communicate leadership by leading. When I entered the apartment to meet Wally for the first time, he ran up to me and bit me on the hand. It was a warning bite and just barely broke the skin. I figured Wally needed to know who is boss, but he already knew.

His owner was the boss. My face glowed with embarrassment, and my hand throbbed with pain, as I attempted, awkwardly, to get tough with the little dog in front of his owner. Wally taught me always to bring a treat when visiting a new client's home.

CHAPTER ONE MY PHILOSOPHY

I developed my dog philosophy from two basic ideas. First, most people need to improve their leadership skills. Second, each dog is unique and requires a training approach tailored to him. Teaching a dog is too personal to be packaged into a "one size fits all" method. However, what every method of training has in common is that the owner must become a leader. The average dog owner wants to do what is best for his dog but isn't interested in becoming an expert trainer. My philosophy will help you be the leader your dog will want to obey.

I will encourage you to become more direct, enthusiastic, forgiving, and loving. Dogs generally possess enormous amounts of these coveted traits. Observing dogs has assisted me in nurturing these characteristics in my personal life. The result? I've developed wonderful new friendships with dogs—and humans, too!

The two most common questions that dogs owners ask are: "How do I teach my dog to do something?" and "How do I stop it from doing other things?"

BE
DIRECT

Use only positive reinforcement to teach your dog to obey commands so it will look forward to pleasing you.

Don't roll your eyes when your dog behaves badly. Let him know his behavior displeases you by being direct with him every single time he demonstrates it. He learns that each time he does this certain thing, your response makes him uncomfortable. Scold him while he is committing the unwanted behavior. This is being direct; to scold him after the fact is not, and will only confuse him. Immediately after scolding him, praise him for complying. Firmly say, "Don't jump on me!" Get him off you. Then say "Thank you."

BE
ENTHUSIASTIC

Dogs respond to energy and enthusiasm. They do not care for overly cool teachers. Sing a happy song, do a little dance, it will trigger a dog's attention. Be especially enthusiastic when teaching new tricks and commands. Use enthusiasm as a reward and your dog will really look forward to obeying you. However, if you give a constant flow of enthusiasm, he will not recognize it as praise for a particular behavior. Give your dog work to perform and reward his efforts with enthusiastic words, food, and physical attention.

Being enthusiastic with a dog in the privacy of my home is one thing, but out in the street it can be awkward. I am afraid of looking silly in public. Dogs taught me that it is good to be excited about life, and I began to practice expressing a wider range of feelings by praising (and scolding) dogs in public places. Now, I am better able to express my emotions with people, too.

HERB RITTS

TRY FORGIVENESS

Dogs have an enormous capacity for forgiveness. Most will forgive ignorance, and even cruelty, from their leaders, within seconds of the offense. Dogs don't hold a grudge with a friend. Their forgiveness will prevail when met half way. This highly evolved characteristic can be mistaken for a sort of masochism, but it is not. Forgiveness is their natural expression of loyalty to the leader. This loyalty is the result of their dependence on the leader, and other pack members, for survival. Most of my dog friends have been saintly in their willingness to forgive, and we should not overlook their example.

Unlike dogs, people must learn forgiveness, because they are usually not so good at it. Being right is often more important than being happy. Every time you reprimand your dog, you must immediately forgive him, give a new command, and praise him for obeying. If your dog doesn't know any commands yet, praise him for ceasing an unwanted behavior. I decided to try this in my human relationships, and it worked there for me, too.

GILLES BENSIMON

REMEMBER
TO BE LOVING

Within any family, there is no more loving member than the dog. Who else is happy to see you at the door, no matter how miserable your day was? Your dog always accepts you despite your sweaty armpits and garlic breath. Who else knows exactly how to treat you when you are devastated by bad news? I learned the secret to happiness by watching dogs. The beauty of dogs is that they make people feel loved no matter what.

Having a dog as a friend makes me feel needed and unconditionally loved; I am always important in my dog's eyes. By example, dogs taught me that the most important possession I have to offer anyone is my time, my company, and my love. Demonstrate love by giving your dog a purpose and work to do. He will feel more comfortable with his place in your "pack" and be happier for it.

FABRIZIO FERRI

LEAD
THE PACK

Animals are not human beings, so their needs are not identical to ours. While this fact is obvious when talking about birds or crocodiles, it is sometimes difficult for dog lovers to admit that difference on an emotional level. For instance, humans dislike being ordered around, but dogs feel secure with a bossy leader. Dogs are hierarchical animals, so if your dog isn't convinced you are the boss, he will be insecure. Dogs want your leadership role to be clearly defined.

I use a dog's own nature to teach him that I'm the leader. I use his territorial nature, his pack instinct, his early life den experience, and his natural cravings for a hierarchy in the way a real top dog would. I lead the hunt for food and water; lead him through doorways; ignore him strategically; name all his toys; and design territorial restrictions in the apartment. I teach him to obey various commands or tricks; I communicate that I'm the leader when we exit my home together by choosing our direction.

"He is going to hate me," you may worry. "It's not my personality to be bossy," some say. People resist leading their dogs for these and other reasons. Nobody wants to deprive his dog of the freedom humans consider so precious. But freedom is a responsibility, and dogs must earn increments of it over time.

Throughout history, humans have put dogs to work and led them. That is how dogs became "man's best friend." Dogs who didn't work hard were tossed out of the pack or house. A dog that has high regard for his owner's leadership will be a better friend.

CHANGE YOUR ATTITUDE ABOUT LEADERSHIP

Realize that being a leader is the most loving way to relate to your dog. Make it important to you, and have fun with it. Teach your dog silly tricks with ridiculous names and laugh with him about it. Leadership doesn't mean "bully." Yes, you must set limits and enforce rules, but your dog needs pats and kisses, too. You are mommy and daddy, his cheering section, his best pal, and his Dean of Students—rolled into one.

A real leader is capable of both praising and reprimanding a dog, but emphasizes the praise. Leaders are not drill sergeants. Nor are they saints with boundless patience. An excellent model for all aspiring leaders is an average New Yorker who has a heart of gold, but won't take any "you know what" from anybody. Dogs relate to this personality type very well because they are never confused about where the leader stands on any matter, large or small.

SEAN ELLIS

DESTINY ISN'T
BLUE

Finding the right puppy can be difficult. Nan Bush and I traveled to three different states examining litters and attending dog shows looking for a male golden retriever puppy. It is both glorious and confusing to be surrounded by thirty puppies while trying to choose one. Nan's boyfriend, Bruce, fell in love with a pup in New Jersey. Nan and I went there to see it and discovered, to our shock, the fattest little creature God dared create. He had wrinkles on top of folds. Nan and I passed him back and forth, laughing our heads off. How could this internationally known photographer have fallen in love with porky squared? Why this pup? Oh well, maybe it was destiny, and anyway, he was the boss.

Three weeks later the puppy was old enough to be delivered to Nan and Bruce's loft in New York City. We were surprised to see the pup's transformation. He was now only fat like a normal pup and very cute. Bruce had put up with three weeks of good-humored teasing and now felt vindicated in his choice. So I devised a new tease—there must have been a puppy switch. Everyone laughed, even Bruce.

After a few days, the breeder called to say we indeed had the wrong pup. It wasn't even the correct sex! The puppy Bruce actually chose would be delivered that afternoon, and according to the breeder, the little female could be picked up for return at the same time. I knew there was no way they were going to return her. If the male pup was the fattest of all, then the female was the luckiest. Living with Nan and Bruce is the best way to be a dog. The search was on for dog names. Bruce has two special talents: He takes a hell of a picture, and he picks the best names for puppies. The female was named Destiny. The male named Blue. They became two of my best friends, but never got to see their eighth birthdays. They died within six months of each other from unrelated illnesses. There is a loud sound when so many hearts are broken at the same time.

CHAPTER TWO CRATE EXPECTATIONS

Wolves are born in underground caves called dens. The mother wolf gives birth and cares for the newborns there. Similarly, the puppies are warm, safe, and comfortable in a den. A den is not a jail on Rikers Island; it is the Bat Cave with cool things to play with. The purpose of the den is to keep him safe from electrical wires, from destroying your furniture with inappropriate chewing, and from peeing all over your home. To properly house train a dog you will need a crate and a corral. Put a bed in the crate, and place it inside of the corral. Create an acceptable place for him to pee and poop on the other end of the corral. Leave the crate door open so he can exit every time he needs to pee.

The pee place in the corral is only good when he is home alone. When you are home together but you are unable to keep an eye on him, lock him in the crate/den so he can't go to the other side of the corral to pee. Take him outside frequently, at least every hour, so he can have many opportunities to "make" in the right place (outside) and receive all the treats and love, which accompany this great success. When he pees on his papers in the corral there is no big reward. With this method he will prefer to do it outdoors.

When at home, allow the pup to follow you from room to room. Use a metal chain leash that he can't chew through to keep a close eye on him while you watch TV. If he indicates a need to pee

(circling and sniffing), you can take him outside. If he begins to mess, it will happen right in front of your eyes. Learn to recognize his indications. Do not interrupt him with a loud noise or become angry, or else he may become inhibited to "make" while you are nearby.

As he gets older and demonstrates an ability to "hold it" you can tether him when you are out of the house. Use a short metal chain (twelve to eighteen inches) attached to an anchor in the floorboard where two walls meet in a corner. The tether allows your dog the same space for moving around as the crate, but he is getting an education on how to behave in your home, without bars. If the tether (chain-length) is the right length, he will resist peeing while attached to it for the same reasons he will resist peeing while in the crate: Dogs prefer to pee and poop away from their sleeping space. But if not properly cared for, dogs will sleep in and even eat their own mess.

I recommend a den/crate inside a corral for pups until six months of age and then tethering when you are out of the house during the next six months. When you are home, your pup should be with you so you can keep a watch over him and create a special bond.

Give your pup a chance to relieve himself at the appropriate times, or he will be forced to mess in your home, in his den/crate, and on the tether. At about the age of four months, he will begin to develop enough muscle control of his bladder to be expected to start trying to hold his urine for increasing lengths of time. Before this age, most pups have no control at all. Never punish puppies for messing in the house. Young pups need to relieve themselves after napping, exercising, drinking water, and eating. Keep track of when he eats and drinks, so you can anticipate his need to pee and poop. Take him out for five-minute "business" walks ten (or more) times a day so he can have lots of opportunities to mess in the right place: outside. Don't roam the neighborhood. Just walk in front of your building, back and forth, so he can find a favorite place. If you walk him for forty minutes, you will be reluctant to take him out as frequently as he needs. When he "makes" during one of these bathroom walks, reward him with a walk around the block and a little play time. Don't exercise him during these walks. Play with him in the apartment or house so he can burn off energy there.

TWO DOGS AND AN ACTOR

Michael Rappaport is a popular movie actor who recently discovered he has a great fondness for dogs. After buying Frankie, a chocolate labrador retriever, he rescued another dog, Stanley, from the streets of Los Angeles. Michael's heart is the size of a watermelon, but you could write what he knew about dogs on a single square of toilet paper. This is where I came in.

He found it difficult sharing his New York City apartment with the two dogs. Frankie was an exuberant puppy, which is always trying on the nerves, and Stanley, the rescue, had some serious fear problems. She required a specific approach aimed at building her confidence and reconditioning her responses to certain situations. Every dog is different and requires a unique training approach. Michael needed to learn my leadership philosophy, two training methods, and lines for his next film. This would require considerable effort from anyone.

After suffering through a fair amount of late-night anxiety about his new housemates, Michael grasped the importance of being a pushy New Yorker with his dogs. He already had the love part down pat. As his confidence grew, so did the happiness in his home.

KAMIL SALAH

CHAPTER THREE
THE ULTIMATE TRAINING SECRET: YOUR VOICE

Use an appropriate tone, when speaking to your dog. When teaching new commands, use only positive intonation. To curb his bad behavior, use the tone of your voice to communicate first disappointment and then joy, within five seconds. Example: You want to set a rule about jumping so he won't make a habit of this obnoxious behavior. When Little Jumper springs up at you, grab hold of him firmly and reprimand him by growling "Don't you dare jump on me." Get him off you; then give him some commands that he can obey ("kiss," "come," or "paw" for instance). And, finally, praise him for complying. A few seconds ago you were removing his paws from your chest and scolding, now you are smiling and praising him for obeying your commands. This method of teaching reminds your dog that you two are a team, but that you are the leader.

ENRIQUE BADULESCU

This method is the most efficient way to communicate your rules and restrictions. His mind grasps information in short time spans. Lessons that take a long time are not direct. It is not confusing to be reprimanded for jumping, and then praised for "coming."

When your dog misbehaves, speak to him about his behavior in a tone of voice that reflects your displeasure. Be firm and tough sounding but not loud. Never yell at your dog. Dogs discipline each other by growling, not by barking. This tone must be recognizably different from the voice you use when he is good. And you must be prepared to switch voices instantly. You may feel awkward expressing yourself in this way with Little Jumper, particularly in public places, but don't allow pride to be an excuse for ignoring the most effective method of communicating with a dog.

Give him plenty of verbal guidance. He will look up at you seeking approval. Thank him for behaving well. If he is to become a good follower, you must tell him what to do. At stairwells, doorways, street corners, and elevators he should look to you for instructions on how to proceed rather than rushing ahead on his own accord with you in tow.

WHISPER
SWEET
NOTHINGS

It is vital to the well-being of your dog that you talk to him in a loving way, with language that has nothing to do with training, leadership or commands. Tell him stories in which he is the hero, sing lullabies, and make him promises about tomorrow. Buy fun toys, make up nicknames for him, and let him earn his favorite snack many times, every day.

Tell your dog about your hopes and dreams so a trust and love develops between you. Tell him your fears and insecurities as a way of figuring out your own mind, and you will feel grateful to him for listening so attentively and patiently. Your heart will become full as you lie on the grass together watching the clouds in the sky become rowboats and roller skates.

Dogs are enthusiastic lovers of people, so who better to teach us lessons about love? Refuse to wait until tomorrow to say "I really love you a lot," and "Please forgive me."

I am teaching you to be bossy with your dog, but I am putting this bossiness into context: We are responsible for providing our dogs with all the love and happiness they will experience in life.

RICHARD PHIBBS

GREEK, LATIN, OR FRENCH. HOW TO TALK TO YOUR DOG

A command he has already obeyed one hundred times doesn't deserve the same energetic praise as a new command. You are probably not giving your dog enough emotion when praising or reprimanding. I recommend you over do it. Don't wait until you're sincerely angry to reprimand him. It is impossible to build a powerful relationship with a dog if you only teach him your rules when you are in a rage. Being furious is a reaction, not a philosophy. Likewise, I expect you probably spoil and make a fuss over him for no reason other than that he looks so darling. Save this enthusiasm for rewarding him when he obeys you. A good leader recreates enthusiasm and disappointment during the moment-to-moment interactions with his dog.

FRANCESCO SCAVULLO

PRAISE HIM

Help your dog to apply meaning to your praise. Tell him why you are praising him. Say "Good Come," rather than "Good Dog." Repeat the word "Come" several times as you praise him. The tone of your praise should be very easy to distinguish from the reprimand tone. Use lots of high-pitched inflections; smile and stroke your dog; clap your hands, and give him a standing ovation. Rub his chest, scratch his neck, and kiss his face while you praise him with words and emotions. Give him food when you praise him, and he will build an even happier association with your praise. I like to sing a little song and do a happy dance because it makes me feel more joyful, and then my praise is more sincere.

MARY ELLEN MARK

COMMAND YOUR TROOPS

When you are teaching your dog a new trick it is best to repeat the command word with a happy, energetic tone so a positive association develops in his mind between the behavior and the word. When you say "Come here," he should smile with his body language.

It is acceptable but not ideal to use a request tone, like a question, when giving commands. "Will you stay, Little Marco Polo?" However, generally a command should be said confidently, as though you really expect it to be obeyed. It is not a mean tone and must be distinguished from a reprimand. Listen to your voice. How do you sound? A command tone is how you would give directions to a lost tourist. "The United Nations? Go down to 42nd Street and turn left."

THOMAS SCHENK

JUST SAY NO

If you own a particularly strong-willed dog, you should avoid using a strong reprimand voice. Instead, remain calm and use a word that means, "Don't do that." I like "uh uh." Say it in a normal tone with no emotion. You do not want to be confrontational with a domineering dog, and a tough tone of voice would be.

Here are the important parts of a verbal reprimand that should be used with most dogs: emotion; drama; facial expression; and tone of voice. The words you say are not as important as snarling your lip, wrinkling your brow, and growling your words. Do not yell; sound disappointed instead. Depending on his personality, this display of emotion will distress your dog to some extent. He will understand you don't accept his current behavior. Learn to create this energy and demeanor in an instant. If you can do this, then he will never have any doubt where you stand on an issue. Never reprimand for more than three seconds. More is unnecessary. And always give commands and praise after every reprimand.

ELLIOTT ERWITT

STAY PLEASE, SKYE!

The stunt made me nervous not because it was dangerous, but because it was my first day as a dog wrangler on the set of a commercial, and I wanted there to be a second. The director asked me to get my dog, Skye, into a rowboat and go to the far side of the pond where another rowboat was tied to a tree. This place was inaccessable by land. Skye was to "Stay" in the second boat by himself as I rowed back to shore and took my place beside the camera. When directed, I would call to him and he'd jump out of the boat and swim toward me. A piece of cake, right? Not really. I never taught him to "Stay" in a boat by himself, although I had taught him to "Stay" in just about every other situation. I wanted to dazzle the director by succeeding immediately with this first stunt, reducing the need for additional "takes," and in doing so, secure more work for myself.

There were other challenges to Skye's success on the first take. The isolated country setting was packed with distractions. There were large event tents, an enormous boom box playing Latin music, photo assistants, camera crew, hair and make-up artists, clothing stylists, models, and art directors from several departments. Skye made best friends with most of the thirty or so people there. Half had secret crushes on him, and the other half had become card-carrying members of his fan club. All these admirers were on my side of the pond, and I knew this would work against his obeying the "Stay" command in a new situation.

As the director yelled "Action!" Skye began to bark. I was mortified. I commanded him to be quiet. The director loved the barking and told me to allow it. A moment later a helicopter appeared. It was carrying the advertising executives, and glided to a landing within fifty yards of where Skye was all alone and trying to perform a good "Stay." I definitely never trained him to tolerate this kind of distraction. Skye performed perfectly despite the hubbub, and I got three days of work.

CHAPTER
FOUR
CUISINE
CUISINE

Use food to convey leadership to your dog. He understands that food is crucial for survival, and he'll look to the leader of the pack for strategies during hunting expeditions. You can either be his waiter or the leader of the hunt. Ask your dog to perform a few commands before giving him breakfast and dinner so he thinks he is earning it. "Eat it up" is a command he will always obey.

Food rewards should always be used to teach new tricks or commands. Use very small pieces of treats that crumble between two fingers so that your Little Starvin' Marvin can continuously look up at you while licking the flavor. Freeze-dried liver is perfect for this, and most dogs love the taste. Encourage eye contact as you dole out the snack and praise him. Don't give him an entire biscuit because he will take it and turn his attention toward the ground to eat it. He may even run off and hide it. If your dog is not motivated by food, then he will probably be obsessed with a particular toy you can use as a reward.

At first, use the treat as a bribe. Show it to him and refuse to give it until he performs for you. As soon as he understands what you are asking of him, he will begin to do it for you without seeing the treat. From this point on, it is no longer a bribe; now it's a reward. He will be interested in learning and obeying your commands so that he can earn your rewards. He will want to obey you, and it will

become a habit for him. Soon after he is expert at the new trick, begin to give him a snack every other time he obeys the command. Continue to teach him new tricks for which he can earn plenty of food rewards.

Please don't be fooled into feeding your dog a strict kibble diet. That would be like giving children an astronaut's meal instead of fresh food. Experiment with all kinds of food. He is an omnivore and can eat most anything, although, some foods will agree with him more than others. Chocolate is not a poison, but avoid giving large amounts. Onions are also not advisable in large quantities, but that doesn't mean a dog should never eat them. And scoffing a chicken bone from the gutter does not require a trip to the emergency room.

I recommend that you do investigate the possibility of feeding your dog a diet of organic, raw vegetables; organic, raw meat; and a high-quality kibble without grain in it.

PAUL JASMIN

A BEAR CAUGHT IN A SPYDER'S WEB

All dogs are different and must be treated as individuals. Kelly called me about her dog, Spyder, who was very young and without any problems. Kelly wanted me to help her to preempt any. Spyder was a wonderful Jack Russell terrier with almond-shaped eyes that coo at you. I never had such an easy job. Spyder was a voracious student and energetic pup. We became fast friends as she learned to work for rewards and affection. She worked hard, and I gave her loads of love and treats. We fell in love quickly. Then one day Kelly, who like her dog, is intelligent, beautiful, and highly energized, told me she was going to buy a second dog. A rare breed she said.

Bear was a miniature Jack Russell terrier; if you can believe such a thing really exists. He was the tiniest little insect of a dog. He is, perhaps, the most precious thing on the planet. But unfortunately for us all, Bear did not share Spyder's energy or enthusiasm for activity. He had a few commands he would gladly obey, but he refused to learn anything that required his straying very far from the nearest lap. The two dogs were as different as apes and ants. It's always difficult for dog owners to accept that what worked well for one dog might not for another. Bear couldn't handle verbal reprimands, he would become confused and stuck. Spyder appreciated verbal guidance about whether or not she was performing well. Bear retreated into an emotional hole when we expected too much from him. Spyder succeeded when pushed to her learning limit.

Spyder

Bear

DIDIER MALIGE

CHAPTER FIVE
DISCIPLINE: SPARE THE ROD, PLEASE

Clients often ask me, "What is an acceptable punishment?" The concept of punishment makes many clients anxious because it implies a beating.

But there is a distinct difference between disicipline and punishment. The dogs themselves taught me that some amount of discouragement and discipline is helpful when it is administered with proper timing. The amount and frequency of the discipline must be determined on an individual basis.

Special considerations should be made for dogs who are young, nervous, fearful, or dominant. Punishing these dogs will be counterproductive or even dangerous. Because you may not have much experience with disciplining dogs, I recommend that you start with the most gentle methods of discouragement.

DEBORAH TURBEVILLE

Many owners have difficulties appropriately disciplining their dogs. Some people punish little; others punish too much, and most use bad timing for discipline. If your preferred method of training requires punishment, then here is your number one rule: Only discipline when Little Khan is beginning to do something bad or in the middle of it. Do not ever punish him afterward. Got it? If you break this cardinal rule, you may diminish your dog's learning capacity and his confidence in your leadership. Never punish him by not speaking to him for twenty minutes; dogs are confused by grudges. Never reprimand him every five minutes for an offense he committed an hour ago. Now that is confusing! Only reprimand him while he is misbehaving, then let go of it. Forgive him. Focus on the fact that he is now complying with you, and his confidence in you will grow.

Some training methods use absolutely no discipline. Dogs trained to assist the handicapped are one example. Those dogs must be allowed to create, invent, and explore. Other methods prohibit leaders from ever speaking harshly to dogs, but require severe physical punishments. The "old" style requires both harsh reprimand (words) and physical punishment. Creating a little discomfort for your dog when he is about to misbehave or during his wrongdoing is an effective form of discipline.

Along with information on developing leadership skills, I am including some training instruction for those of you who have no training method. Some dogs will thrive with a particular method; others will drive their owners to drink. The method I am explaining here should be effective with nearly all moderate-tempered dogs. Keep in mind, there is usually no place for punishment when teaching dogs to perform tricks or commands. Punishment/discouragement is for teaching your dog what not to do. Sometimes it is better to chase squirrels with him instead of holding him back. If you can recreate the circumstances in which your dog is likely to do something you consider "misbehaving," praise and reward him with food BEFORE he reacts to the circumstance. If he begins to react, ignore him, or toss a book on the floor to distract him from the circumstance. Then get his attention again, and praise him for focusing on you.

DISCIPLINE IS NOT NECESSARY FOR MOST DOGS AND SHOULD BE AVOIDED WHENEVER POSSIBLE.

1   Try a verbal reprimand to discourage unwanted behavior. If this method works, there is no reason to try other forms of discouragement.

2   Deprive your dog of a prized possession to discourage his behavior without any physical discomfort.

3   A stream of watered-down lemon juice from a squirt gun can be an effective deterrent with some dogs, while others may consider it a game if they see you doing the squirting. Aim for the mouth. The eyes are off limits.

4   Hold the dog's mouth closed for a few seconds.

5   Toss a big book on the floor to make a loud noise and startle them. They should come to you for comfort.

6   Try a three-minute time out. Wait until Little Al Capone is quiet for five seconds before letting him out so he doesn't think fussing equals freedom. Don't isolate him in his den. It's important that his den does not become associated with discipline and discouragement in his mind.

For many dogs, some small level of physical discipline is acceptable, but it must always be instructional, never vengeful. If I decide it is appropriate, I give small physical discouragements timed exactly to when the dog is misbehaving so he will develop a negative impression toward his behavior. Then I command him to do something, and praise him. The definition of discipline is that it deter the unwanted behavior. Your dog must understand what is not allowed, and discipline effectively discourages him from repeating bad behavior. Experiment to decide which technique works for you and your dog.

If you become violently angry at your dog, lock yourself in the bathroom, splash cold water on your face, and have a conversation with the mirror about who you are, and how you want to live.

BRUCE WEBER

DARK RED SWEETIES

Stuart grew up on a farm in Australia. He always had dogs as a kid, and he continued to own them as an adult. When I met him, he had just received a dark red golden retriever as a gift from one of his clients.

He named the pup Red, and I helped the two of them to get along well. A year later, Stuart decided to get another dark-red golden and named him Max. They were both enthusiastically obedient because I figured out what rewards motivated them. It was difficult for me to resist spoiling them because they were so cute. But I kept their welfare ahead of my impulses and allowed them to work and earn their rewards. Red would swim to China for a gentle caress and a loving word of praise. Max would climb a tree for a toss of the ball. There is no need for discipline if you know what motivates a dog.

I trained them to obey properly while in the company of other dogs at the dog run, which was beside the Franklin Deleno Roosevelt Highway. I perfected their ability to heel off the leash amidst the traffic, pigeons, stray cats, and screaming kids on bikes.

I always fancied the three of us an impressive trio, breaking all the safety rules, off leash, walking up First Avenue, the red dogs at a perfect heel.

JAMES CALDERO

CHAPTER SIX

WORK YOUR DOG CAN DO

Dogs have performed work for humans since the dawn of their friendship with us thousands of years ago. A dog's bark served as one of our first alarm systems. Eventually, we bred dogs so they could specialize in certain kinds of work, such as tracking, herding, and retrieving. The unique alliance between man and dog is founded on a history of teamwork, performance, and results. Empathy and mutual affection exist between us because we are both social creatures who will sacrifice for family and friends.

It is part of a dog's nature to work for his family. What sort of career do you have in mind for your little lap dog? If your answer is "none," then he's unemployed and not as happy as he could be. Work gives his life purpose and direction. Don't condemn him to waiting for the postman to bring the bills. Obeying you is his job. Love, praise, food, and games are his paycheck.

Work can be fun. For example, try a scent game I call "Find It." Sit on the couch facing Little Gallileo with some pieces of his favorite treat in your breast pocket. Show him one of these treats and then

ALEXIS RODRIGUEZ - DUARTE

put it beside you on the couch. Let him see that your hand is now empty, and repeatedly ask him to find it. He will probably be confused because in the past you have always placed the treat into his mouth. He may need a hint to find where you put the treat although it is so ridiculously obvious to you. Make it easy for him to find it the first few times because it is best for him to succeed and have fun in new games and lessons. When he eventually finds the treat, allow him to eat it, and praise him with, "Good find it, my friend, find it, is a good find it, find it, find it."

Hide the snack in the same place three or four times in a row. Then place it in a slightly more difficult place, behind you, for example. He'll immediately go to the first hiding place, so be sure to assist him if he needs it. Don't get discouraged if he learns slowly. Each dog learns tricks at his own pace. This game is excellent because as he progresses, you are honestly excited.

The "Find It" game is also an opportunity to practice "stay." While you hide a ball or treat, have him "go to your bed" and, "stay" in the various positions (down, sit, stand). Make him "stay" until you command him to "find it boy." Practicing "stay" can be boring, but combining it with the "Find it" game lends it a purpose and gives your dog more opportunity to work for you. Over time, hide the snack in increasingly complicated places, and let your Little Ponce De Leon earn your praise by finding it.

NAME EVERYTHING

What other work can I give my dog? Your dog will answer this question. He does all sorts of things on his own initiative. Observe these activities and name them. Since he likes to eat, turn it into a command. By naming things he instinctively cares about, you will condition him to care about your leadership. If he enjoys licking your face, call it "Kiss." Urinating becomes "Do a pee pee." Barking is "Sing." Jumping up can become "Dance with me." Every time you put his leash on before a walk say, "Saddle up." Be creative.

Your dog can learn perhaps a hundred commands, so don't bore him to death with the same six every time. Name everything he interacts with so you can instruct him frequently. A well-trained dog enjoys obeying you. A successful half-hour training session doesn't mean he is good for the other 23.5 hours of the day. Don't only practice with your dog; live with him. Every interaction communicates something, and therefore, is a form of training. Constantly ask yourself, "What is he learning about me now?"

Show him his toy and become excited. Say, "It's your ball" repeatedly in a happy tone. Give him a treat as well. Then hide the ball behind your back and become a museum figure. Go from cheerleader to deadpan a few times and your dog will understand that the item is called "ball" and that it is special.

STEWART SHINNING

Teach him to distinguish one treat from another by naming each of them. Put a piece of cheese in one fist and some salami in the other, and tell your dog to "Find the cheese." When he goes to the correct hand give it to him and say "cheese" a few times. When he nudges the wrong hand, say "ugh ugh, find the cheese" and refuse to give him any reward.

These methods work with all kinds of items (and people), but I suggest you only name things you want him to interact with, such as toys, snacks, dog friends, human friends, the leash, and his bed. If your dog turns out to be a sharp cookie, you can name things he should never go near or do. This includes the kitty litter, poop in the park, food on the street, your glasses, and shoes. If you are using discouragement, do so in these situations.

You need an additional command for occasions when you don't want him to interact with something at this particular moment, but in general, it would be acceptable. "Leave it!" means "Not now," whereas "No" means "Never."

LEAVE IT

What makes a dog obedient? Isn't it as much his willingness to not commit certain acts, as it is his ability to perform commands? Use "Leave it" when he's about to do something you don't want him to. It doesn't matter what it is. If you are not in the mood or you don't have the time, you can tell him to leave it alone. This command includes greeting other dogs, strangers, a baby carriage, urinating on objects, and so on.

Place some food on the floor in front of your unleashed dog, and say, "Leave it" as you prevent him from gobbling it up. Place yourself between him and the treat, stomp your foot, push him away, what ever it takes. Do this until he chooses to control himself, and praise him with "Good leave it." When he willingly behaves himself, pick up the food and feed it to him as a reward and say, "OK, eat it up."

Next, put a few of his favorite toys on the living room floor, along with a remote control, and your favorite sunglasses. Without the leash, walk him past the items. If he reaches down for one of your things, say "Leave it", and stomp your foot on the ground. He will probably stop and look up at you with a quizzical expression. Praise him because he obeyed, "what a good leave it!" If he reaches for one of his own toys, praise him with "yes, that's your ball," as you repeat the name of it.

Do not allow him to have many toys on the floor at the same time. You are not his toy slave. Give him a chew toy and a play toy and put all the others in a box. Exchange them a few times a day so you are the manager of the toys.

Charcoal and
friend. 1950 TUXEDO
N.Y. Peter Beard

SING, LITTLE PAVAR'OTTI

Teach your dog to bark on command. His barking is evidence of an aptitude for using his voice. He probably makes several different sounds, all of which should be named. It may seem contradictory, but the best way to decrease a barking problem is to turn it into a command. Don't suppress his natural activities; give them context.

Barking at the door is partly an instinct to protect the territory and the pack. The doorbell, a friend in a weird hat, or a noise in the hallway, all may trigger this instinct. It can be frightening to your guests, annoying to your neighbors, and a real pain in the ear to the owner who lives with a dog whose barking is out of control. If your dog is not convinced of your rank, he will tend to feel more responsible for the territory. Teach him rules about barking so it has a context. Two or three barks at the front door are good. This is work for him to do. Now that he has informed you someone is there, you can take control of the situation.

Praise him when he barks with an excited tone of voice and the command word "Get him." This word may prove helpful if you ever feel threatened by a stranger who won't know that your dog is merely singing. Feel free to use any command word that suits you, like all my commands, "Get him" is merely a suggestion. When he barks for any reason during the next few days, you will encourage him. Say "Get him, boy, good get him" repeatedly and enthusiastically. After a few days, he will bark on command. Next, you will teach him to stop barking on command. Have him "Get him" and then interrupt him by saying "Quiet" in a firm voice with a mean face. Reach down and close his mouth if that is what it takes to get results, but don't forget to smile and praise him once he has quieted. Give a little snack. If soon after he starts to bark again, repeat the whole routine. He will soon bark and cease barking on command. If he violates your limits about barking (too much or wrong situation), you can command him to be "Quiet."

OPEN YOUR HEART AND PLAY

Puppies develop senses of the pack through playing together. Their instincts are honed and bonds are formed. Their brains are developing and play aids the process. They learn that being bitten hurts, and to avoid aggression with their elders. An adult dog needs to play too, so don't be too stuffy to enjoy having fun with him. You will create a special bond that may compare favorably to the other things that interest him.

Decide when play begins and end it with a command such as "Wanna play, Sugar?" Be properly dressed when you give this command because playing is messy, and you don't want a little dirt to ruin it.

Play hide and seek, fetch, find, and chase me. These games are fun, so your dog sees you as a fascinating boss. Other games like wrestle and tug-of-war, and allowing him to jump on you can put rebellious notions in the heads of strong-willed dogs. Chasing your dog is a game you should resist until he has proven his competence at coming when called. If your dog seems to become less obedient after you play certain games, avoid those activities.

Name each game to increase your dog's vocabulary. Games are work that he is enthusiastic about performing. "Fetch" is great fun and excellent exercise. Each time you throw the ball, command him to "Get the ball" and praise him for chasing after it. If he picks it up, begin to encourage him to "Bring

PAMELA HANSON

MIKE PELZMAN

it here" while he approaches you. When he arrives at your feet command him to "Drop it."
MANY DOGS WILL BRING A BALL, BUT NOT DROP IT. NEVER CHASE HIM
TO GET THE BALL BACK. HERE ARE SOME OPTIONS:

1   Have a second ball handy.
2   Ignore him until he drops it.
3   Run away from him so he chases you, and then grab hold of him.
4   Give him the "Come" command.
5   Teach him to "take," "hold," and "release" objects.

"Chase me" is a good game/command because it encourages him to follow and come to you. The very simple game of "Hide and Seek" is an excellent way to demonstrate your leadership during play time, and it entrenches his desire to be near you. Toss a treat on the floor and go hide while he is after the snack. Occasional noises will help him find you, give him a snack when he does. Play these games when you are alone together. Make up fun and creative names for them so they are fun for you, and have the time of your life.

When you're ready to end a game, you may face a bit of resistance from your riled-up pup. Lower your energy and voice, take hold of him and say, "Shhh, its over." He will mirror your energy. Put him through his paces and routine, "Come, Down, Stay, Sit, Kiss, Paw, Sing," and re-establish your rank in the happy pack.

LET'S GO

"Let's go" is permission to proceed, and follow you. Walk from room to room saying, "Let's go" in a happy voice as he follows you. Stop occasionally and touch him affectionately, praise him, give a snack, and then stand up straight again and say, "OK, let's go," and start walking.

In real life, you will use "Let's go" all the time with an adult dog. When you are ready to leave the park, cross the street, enter or exit an elevator, or climb the next flight of stairs. Use it when you are ready to end a visit with another leashed dog on the street. First say, "Let's go," to indicate he should follow you, and then command him about how to follow. Do you want him at a strict "Heel," or a more loose "Easy," which means he can walk a little behind, ahead or away from your side without the kind of focus Heel requires. Don't allow him to cross in front of you while in the "Easy" position. Neither should he loop around behind you to get on your right side. He must remain on your left side just like with "Heel," but he is permitted more freedom.

CHAPTER SEVEN
THE BASIC COMMANDS

All dog owners are dog trainers. Even kids manage to communicate "Sit" to their dogs. You can, too. The system used to instruct your dog to "Sit" can be used for any other trick you care to teach. This is how I do it: Give him the verbal command "Sit," then gently guide his backside with one of your hands. Your other hand goes underneath his chin and guides him up. When the dog sits, give him a treat while you praise him with a "Good sit."

Progressively lessen the pressure you apply to his backside and chin as he shows signs of understanding what you expect of him. Just touch him enough to indicate movement rather than guiding his butt all the way to the ground. You will be initiating the motion, and he will decide to complete it.

Here is another method. Hold a treat in front of his face so that he is looking straight ahead at it, and move the treat slowly over his head toward his tail. He will raise his head to follow the treats and his butt will naturally lower. If needed, apply a small amount of push-down pressure on his rump.

Don't expect him to remain at "Sit" for long periods. That would be "Stay." Praise him for putting his rump on the floor even if it only spends two seconds there.

SIMON SAYS STAND

"Stand," means being on all four feet and keeping still. It is useful at the vet's office, the groomer's, or while being dried after a dip in the pool. Have your Little Leonardo "Sit" and "Stay" at your heel. Turn to face him, take hold of his collar with your right hand, and say "Stand," then pull him forward by the collar (out of "Sit"). At the same time, place your left hand in front of his hind leg to prevent him from walking off. He is now in the "Stand" position. Implied in "Stand" is "Stay," not move, remain frozen on all four. If he takes a step, or sits down, then you urgently express your disapproval, put him back into the "Stand," and praise him. You must always eventually release him from this command by saying "All done."

FRANCESCO SCAVULLO

SIMON SAYS COME

There are many reasons your dog won't "Come." He may not do what you want because you have been an ineffective leader. He may want you to chase and play with him. Or he may be distracted by something more interesting than you. He may be afraid of you because you have hit him in the past for not coming when called.

"Come" is the most important command of all because it ensures control of the dog when he is off the leash. He can have more freedom if he comes when called. You must always praise him when he eventually comes even if you are angry that he ignored you for five minutes. If you scold him when he finally comes, he will make a negative association to the command. Be direct.

Teach the "Come" command to a very young pup by squatting down into a catcher's position and encouraging him to come to you. He will obey because young pups are very needy. Any dog will learn it if you have a friend go to the other side of the living room with a hand full of treats, and the two of you call the dog back and forth. Say "come here, honey bun," and when he gets to you, gently grab hold of his collar, praise and feed him. You must first get hold of his collar so you have control over him, then reward him.

Always use this command before giving him his meals, before going out for a walk, before giving him his toys, and before issuing other commands. Give him more food, more often for obeying "Come." Give him a little playtime with his favorite toy, too. It must be his favorite thing in the world because you are adding distractions to tempt him to ignore you.

DERRICK SANTINI

SIMON SAYS STAY

Start in a small room so you don't need a leash to control him. Have your Little Anchor "Sit" at your heel, give him the "Stay" command, and slowly step away from him, but not straight ahead as if you were going for a walk. Instead, step off to the side with your right foot and slowly drag your left foot until you are standing with your feet together again. He won't understand what is going on and will try to follow you. Now you can teach him what not to do. Do not reprimand him intensely. Instead, create an indignant urgency in your voice, but not anger, "Ugh, ugh" and take him back to his original place, facing in the same direction. Again command him to "Stay" and slowly step away with a smile. Move slowly so he doesn't reflexively follow you. As long as he stays, praise him in a continuous, soft, and happy voice. Use a low-energy tone of voice because if you are too "big," he may be compelled to come to you for some affection and food. Have him "Stay" for ten seconds, then go back to where he is and give snacks. Again command him to "Stay," and step away again. Return frequently with a snack. Don't travel too far away. Repeat this a few times, and then finish by returning to him and saying, "OK, all done" as a release from "Stay." Explode with praise, "Yes, we are all done, you are so smart," and throw his favorite toy. He'll like the work you do together.

As he progresses with "Stay," remaining still for longer periods, you should slowly introduce variations of it. For instance, walk around him in a circle. He will want to keep an eye on you, and might stand up from "Sit" in order to keep you in front of him at all times. He should only move his head to watch you.

Next, step into another room for a moment so that he can't see you. His jingling dog tags will alert you to whether or not he might be leaving "Stay."

Slowly increase the duration in a way that allows him to feel like a success instead of pushing him beyond his limits too soon and failing repeatedly. But every time he breaks the "Stay," you must reposition him in the exact spot he had been in. Do all this work in your home until he is good at it. Add distractions, like toys and food tossed on the floor. Graduate to outdoors where there will be more distractions. Outdoors, you can tie a long rope to his leash and safely put a substantial distance between you.

He will learn to "Stay" in any position you tell him to, whether it is "Sit stay," "Down stay," or "Front paws up on the wall and stay." These are different from each other, and you need to make time to teach him the various positions. Teach one new trick at a time. More than one in the same lesson will confuse him.

Never tell your dog to "Stay" when you are leaving the house to go to work. You don't really expect him to "Stay" for ten hours do you? He will eventually break the "Stay" without your permission and you will have, in effect, taught him to ignore your commands. You must always release him from a "Stay" with "Ok, all done!"

SIMON SAYS DOWN

TO GET YOUR DOG TO LIE DOWN, TRY THE FOLLOWING:

1 Hold a snack between his front paws, but don't let him have it until he gets "Down" for it. This may take a long time if he thinks you are a weak leader, so be patient. If he is not so interested in food then skip a meal so that your snack will have greater value to him during this lesson.

2 Have him "Sit" and gently put one hand on his rump. Use your other hand to slide his front paws out into the "Down" position. Do this on a wooden, or otherwise slippery floor, rather than on a carpet.

3 Try steps 1 and 2 after playing in the park for an hour on a warm Saturday. Exhaustion will compel him to lie down for you.

4 Every time he lies down on his own accord, you can praise him for it from across the room. Make it appear as if there is a connection between his actions and your words.

5 If you put aggressive energy into forcing him down, he will resist you. Even if you have to manipulate him into the "Down," you must give him rewards as though he were obeying perfectly.

Repetition is the key to any lesson your pet is having trouble grasping. Be patient and enthusiastic, and always give a reward when he succeeds. Once he is no longer baffled, you should stop the repetition. Don't bore him or drive him crazy by doing "Down" twenty times in a row. He will be good at 'Down' if you make it fun for him. Have him lie down before each toss of the ball when playing fetch.

6   When he is "Down," have him "Stay" and stand tall above him. Step over him and pause so that you are straddling him with one foot on either side of his body. This is a leadership position. If he is resisting you, increase your bossiness. He needs opportunities to earn your praise. Make your praise more attractive. Do not give him a lot of love without his earning it.

SIMON SAYS HEEL

Heel is a command that means your dog should remain close to your heel. Cooperative dogs only require a buckle collar. You can use a popular devise called a Gentle Leader to prevent pulling, but it doesn't teach heel. That is your job.

THE FOLLOWING EXERCISES WILL HELP HIM GRASP WHAT HEEL MEANS:

1   Keep a treat in your left hand as a lure to have him at the perfect position. Praise him as you walk and periodically give him a small piece of the treat.

2   A beloved toy in your pocket will prevent him from heeling a step in front of you. If he tries to grab at the toy, tell him to leave it.

3   Walk with him beside a wall so he will heel closer to you.

4   It is helpful to heel your dog on the curb of a street where there are no parked cars so you can teach a tighter heel. If he steps into the gutter, you can teach him that you don't want him to be in the street unless you command him to.

5   Command him to heel as you step out into a normal walking pace. Take two steps and then stop. He also should stop on his own in order to remain at your side. Chances are you will have to stop him the first few times by holding the leash taut with your left hand. Do not jerk him in this lesson. Just restrain him with the leash. As soon as you come to a halt by restraining him, create slack in the leash so he is choosing to remain at your heel. Praise, feed him, take three steps, and stop. "Good Heel." One step and stop. "Nice heel." This lesson is excellent for helping him figure out that heel is a place, a position, right beside you.

6   Have him "Heel" at different speeds. A slow jog is a more comfortable pace for him than your normal walking pace is. Jog for twenty steps; resume walking, then slow down to nearly a crawl. Then speed up again, all the while praising him for his "Good heel." Without jerking, use the leash to guide these sudden speed changes, but be sure to avoid keeping a taut leash. Is he deciding to follow you at the various paces you set? Talk to him encouragingly so he looks at you for love, guidance and food. If he is not paying attention to you, he may not be ready to stop or turn when you do.

THESE NEXT LESSONS ARE FOR DOGS WHO KNOW HOW TO "STAY."

7   Have him "Sit" at your heel and command him to "Stay." Take a single step forward. After a few seconds, command him to join you by saying, "Heel," and he should come to your side. Repeat this a few times with him on the leash. Your leash is four feet, your arm is two-and-one-half feet, that means you can safely put six-and-one-half feet of distance between you and your dog, and then he can get to your heel.

8   Have him "Sit" and "Stay" in front of you, facing you. Command him to "Heel" and assist him in wrapping around behind you to get to your left heel. It doesn't matter whether he wraps around you to get there or if he simply goes to your left side and then turns around to face in the same direction as you.

THE EARLY RISERS

Training is about creating a good relationship, so don't hand your dog over to a trainer. Do the job yourself. Pay the trainer to guide you. Otherwise, you will end up like my client-turned-friend, Stanley. He hoped his dogs would obey him if I trained them. I assured him it would be difficult for his dogs to view him as a competent leader if they compared him to me. He insisted, and I needed the job.

Stanley is a gentle pediatrician who owns two wonderful and vivacious mixed breeds, Giorgio and Timothy. These two dogs raise hell everywhere they go. However, when they are with me, they are perfect gentlemen. Stan spoils them, and that is fine. However, he also deprived them of leadership and a sense of purpose.

After a couple years of living together, they began to deprive Stanley of sleep by insisting to go out at three in the morning. He asked me to teach him a few ways to renegotiate his relationship with his "Little Angels." As soon as he became involved in their training he gained enough control over them to guarantee a good night's sleep.

KELLY KLEIN

CHAPTER EIGHT
TEACH HIM ON THE HOME TURF

Teach new commands and tricks in your living room, where there is a small number of distractions, and your dog's attention can be entirely on you. By gradually increasing the distractions, you can expect him to successfully obey commands in more chaotic environments.

Learning commands around other dogs is usually the greatest distraction a dog can face and should be considered the ultimate test area for behaving well. Be warned, if you begin to teach "Stay" for the first time in front of other dogs instead of at home, your dog will be too distracted to learn efficiently. He'll fail repeatedly, and you'll both be discouraged. You might mistakenly decide your dog is stupid and make fun of him, by engaging in unintentional negativity. "Yeah, I love him, but he isn't too bright." Dogs know when you feel this way, and it adds to the impression that you are not a leader. Leaders make followers feel important.

USE THESE DISTRACTIONS:

1. Turn on the radio and television while you give him his various commands.

2. Open all the windows.

3. Have him "Stay," and roll a dime across the floor. If he chases it, reprimand him, return him to the "Stay," and praise him.

4. Toss food on the floor and praise him when he resists going after it.

5. Have friends juggle a ball while you call Little Bozo to "Come."

6. Pretend to throw a ball, in slow motion first, and then normal speed, while giving commands.

7. Open the front door while the dog is at "Stay."

8. Have a dog friend visit you with his owner while your dog obeys you. His reward is a play session.

CHAPTER NINE TERRITORY

Dogs instinctively define their territory for survival and security. Be the supervisor of your home so your dog will respect you. Among the many possible rules indoors is this old favorite, "No dogs on the furniture." However, we will add a modern twist—"Unless invited."

Dogs are not allowed on the furniture because of territorial control, not hyper cleanliness. But I enjoy inviting a dog on the couch with me when I'm watching a video. Decide when your dog may and may not get on the couch by making it a command, "On the couch." If he joins you there without having been invited, reprimand him, and get him off. When he is off, praise him.

If you want him on the couch, and he anticipates your invitation, first get him off and have him perform a command. After he obeys, command him to get "On the couch" a moment later. He will be impressed that his pack leader manages the territory so well.

Don't let Little Precious determine where you get to sit when you are both heading for the couch. Make him move for you. If you allow him to have his own place on your furniture, he may be distressed when your guests need to sit there.

NOE DEWITT

THE MATTRESS QUEEN

If you want your Little Dust Mop to sleep in the bed with you, then do what I suggested for the couch. Do not permit him to sleep on your pillow or near your head. He must always be laying down while on your bed.

The bed belongs to you, and your dog has zero say in whether or not you allow him to sleep there on any given night. If you are married and have a large enough bed, it is fine to let him bed down with you regularly. If you are a single person, be aware that he may become annoyed when you have a pajama party. Your Little Romeo won't be welcome in your bed on that night, will he? He may feel left out or confused and become jealous or protective.

LAURA RESEN

REIGN
THE DOMAIN

Decide upon an area where the dog can't go. The bathroom and the kitchen are good choices even if you have used these places in the past to restrict Little Magellan's mobility. Walk into the bathroom. He follows. If he doesn't follow, then sing a happy tune and do a silly dance, but do not command him to follow you. You don't ever want to ask him to "Come" to you and then punish him for obeying. When he initiates crossing the threshold of the bathroom, shoo him out passionately and intensely. Say, "Go away" or "Back up," or anything else that feels passionate. The moment he has retreated to the other side of the threshold, you should begin to praise him with "Good go away, my boy." Be effusive but stay in the bathroom and keep some distance between you. If he crosses the threshold again to receive a kiss and a pet from you, then scold him and shoo him out again. If he puts even one foot on the threshold to re-enter, reprimand him. When he retreats, praise him. He will catch on quickly if you are consistent and emphatic.

I know imposing this limitation for your Little Nomad may be difficult on an emotional level, but this action will teach him you are a leader worth listening to.

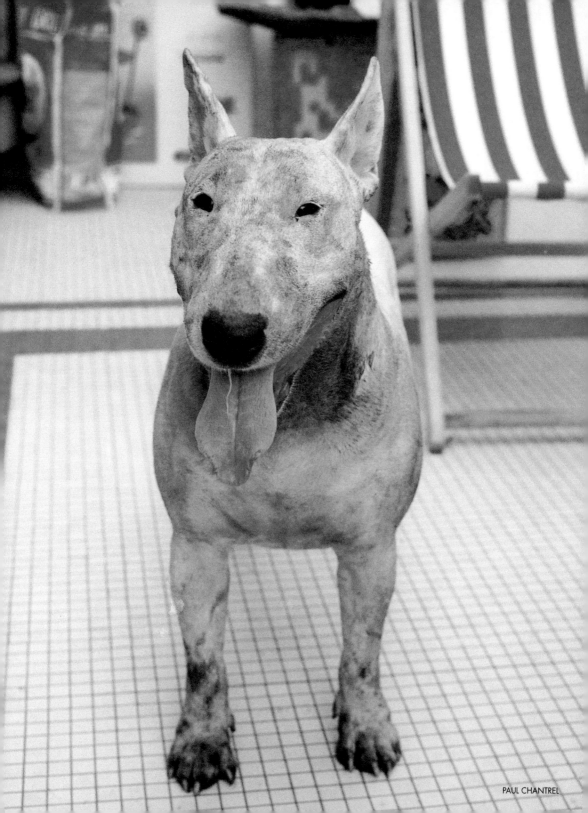

PAUL CHANTREL

MASTER OF THE UNIVERSE

Leaving the house provides an opportunity to communicate leadership. As you grasp the doorknob, your dog is ready to rush out, leaving you behind. You are not his personal doorman. Take a moment at the door to show him you are in charge. Open the door just enough to tempt him to escape but not enough to get his nose out. Command him to "Wait." Move him aside with your leg and position yourself in front of him. Slowly open and close the door a few times while making him wait. Finally, command him to "OK, let's go." He will passionately obey you. Repeat this at the elevator or stairwell.

Be in charge of the territory outdoors as well. He may pee a small amount in fifty different places to mark his presence in the neighborhood. Limit his effort to tinkle on every upright object. Most dogs have a place where they pee immediately upon arriving outdoors. This routine is good and should be encouraged. You will limit the next forty-nine pees. Tell your adult dog when he may and may not pee. Deny him his second, third and forth efforts, and then give him permission on the fifth attempt. Guide him to a lamp post and tell him, "Ok, pee pee here." When he finishes and tries to walk away, don't follow him. You decide when to leave the lamp post. The next time he tries to drag you toward a tree, refuse to follow, tell him to "Leave it."

STEVEN KLEIN

Have him pause, or "Wait" at every street corner. Do not insist that he "Sit" because the hot, cold, or wet weather may make sitting unpleasant for him. Whenever you cross the street, have him "Heel." The street is dangerous, and "Heel" creates the safest position for him. This also presents many opportunities to use the heel command in real-life situations. Upon reaching the other corner, command him to "Easy."

Make him get out of your way and watch out for your feet, rather than you always darting out of his way. If you have a party at home, he will be safer if he is alert to where people are. He will also be safer on a crowded city sidewalk. Stomp your foot on the ground and say "Move." This will wake him up to his surroundings straight away. He hears the sounds your feet make because he is down there near them. The chances of tripping over him go down dramatically when each of you is aware of the other.

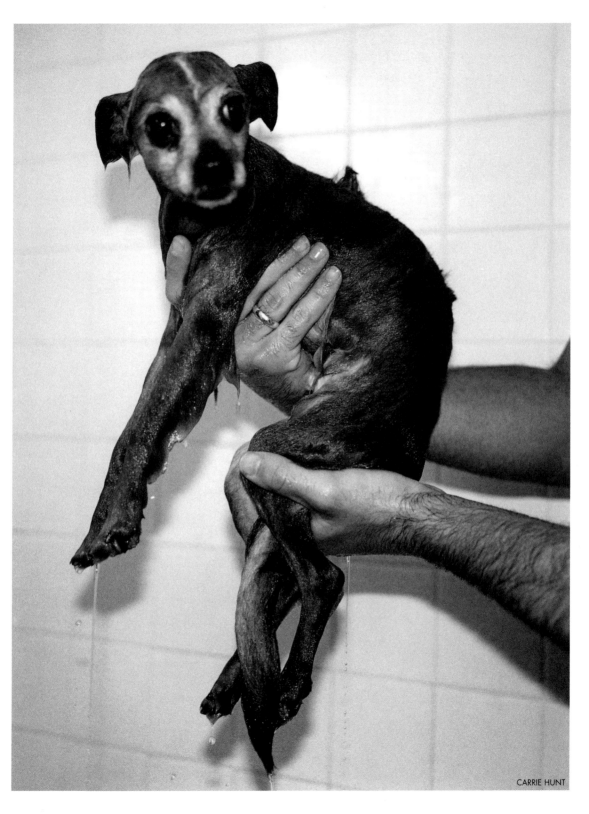

CHAPTER TEN
THE FIX IS IN, SO DO IT

Breeding dogs is a serious undertaking. Leave it to professionals who love a particular breed and have committed their lives to perpetuating that breed's qualities. They sell the offspring of their champion show dogs and, we hope, will be more responsible as breeders than the average dog owner because they have their reputations at stake. The rest of us should prevent our dogs from making puppies because there are already too many unwanted pups languishing in dog pounds in need of loving homes.

If you want your dog to have puppies so your children can witness the miracle of life, then buy a video. If you think you can make some easy money mating your dog with another that isn't a champion show dog, think again. The time, labor, and expense make breeding an unprofitable hobby. If you simply want your dog to "get some tail," then go see a psychologist and get your ego in check. Neuter your pets so they will not create more unwanted dogs for the world to cry over. It is not easy to find good homes for a litter of pups. The shelters and pounds are filled with purebred dogs (as well as every mix imaginable) that suffer miserable lives and are then killed. Moreover, if you do find six good homes for your makeshift litter, then six puppies at the pound have lost the opportunity to be saved.

FRANK W. OCKENFELS III

Forty thousand unwanted dogs and cats are killed in New York City every year. People convince themselves they will care for the offspring of their pets. But what about the grandpuppies and the great-grandpuppies? Did I say forty thousand are killed? Imagine for a moment a pile of forty thousand dead animals. Don't argue about this, have your pets fixed when the vet tells you to, and be proud that you're not making the nightmare even worse. When you bought this book, you made a small donation to help the plight of homeless cats in the New York City area. I love the idea of a dog book benefiting cats, and decided to donate a portion of my personal proceeds to City Critters Inc., an organization that needs financial help to rescue and find good homes for stray cats. It is a group of extremely committed volunteers who donate their own time and money to neuter New York City's cats. Despite the discounted services of generous and kindhearted veterinarians, City Critters has too much work to do and not enough money to do it. Animal homelessness and abuse are major problems that the local government is not doing enough to remedy. City Critters takes direct action to decrease the suffering of animals. They need our support. Please adopt a dog or a cat, or send a tax-deductible contribution to:

CITY CRITTERS, INC.
PO BOX 1345 CANAL ST. STATION
NY, NY 10013-0877
OR CALL 212-252-3183

First published in the United States of America in 2001
by UNIVERSE PUBLISHING
A Division of Rizzoli International Publications, Inc.
300 Park Avenue South
New York, NY 10010

© 2001 Breon O'Farrell

2000 2001 2002 2003 2004 2005 / 10 9 8 7 6 5 4 3 2 1

Designed by Carrie Hunt
Printed in Singapore

Front Cover Photograped by Bruce Weber
Back Cover Photographed by Henry Horenstein

Library of Congress Catalog Card Number: 00-111856

MICHEL COMTE

SPECIAL THANKS TO

My great love Marta, and my little love Simone. My dear friends Bruce Weber
and Nan Bush who know how it feels to help other People's dreams come true. My talented
and hard-working art director Carrie Hunt. Stuart Cameron introduced me to the publisher.
My parents Barbara and Martin, my brothers Bill Jennings and Paul Schulze.
My sisters Dana and Deirdre. My friends and agent Clyde Kuemmerle, Lucy and Sophie.
Manny, Vickie and Dean Barrios, Irene Christopher, Adrian Vargas, Leonard Bruno,
the editor Gena Pearson. Skye, Sea Bensimon and her little sister Thaddeus, Leslie Lambert, Jeanine
Morick and Lil Bouvier. Michael, Nicole and Julian Rappaport, Sandy Carlson,
Miles Cederquist, Elizabeth Arlene, the memory of Wilbur and Winston. Alison and Zach,
Sara, Neowyn and Elbreon, Christiana and Luciano, Maria Chiara and Alessandro, Paolo, Neri
and Michele, bis nonno Renato and bis nonna Gisella, Enrico, zio Pio, Susanna, Sara and Corven.
Palimino and my artist group members. Giovanni C. Russo, and No11.
The memory of Barbara Dewitt. The many helpful and friendly agents, studio assistants
and archivists. Their positivity made a big difference when I was scared to ask for help.
Eddie at Comte, Wendel at Demarchelier, Jessica at Newton, Lauren at Erwitt,
Michelle at Ockenfels, Diana at Watson, Nicolas-Serres-Cousine, Meredith at Mark,
Andrea, Kathryn and Candice Marx at Art Partner, Thomas Bonnouvrier, Melody Brynner, Rain,
Polar Bear, Brian Ferrera, Emma at Santini, Aster at Verglas, Bettina at JGK, Arezu Javan, Alison
Hunter at Katie Barker Agency, Michael, Jeff and Fiona at Leibovitz, Barbara Von Schreiber, Sara
at Shinning, Tico Torres, Kellie Lindsey at Marek Associates,
Ashley at Meisel, Reed Williams, Ingrid and Johanna at Klein, Pamela Sunshine, Vicki and Isabelle
Dwight, Chelsea Black and White Printing Labs, Bico and my itty bitty Little Bear,
Scout, Tug, and the memory of the Bird Dog. To the great dog lovers Tatjana Patitz, C.Z Guest, Etta
James, Diane Keaton and Isabella Rossellini. My last thanks go to the unreasonably
large number of dogs I have known, taught, and learned from.

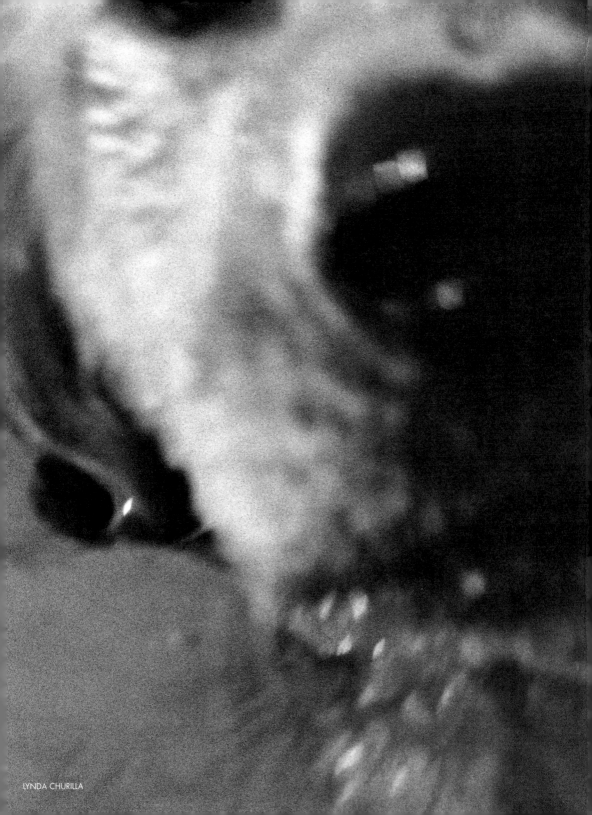